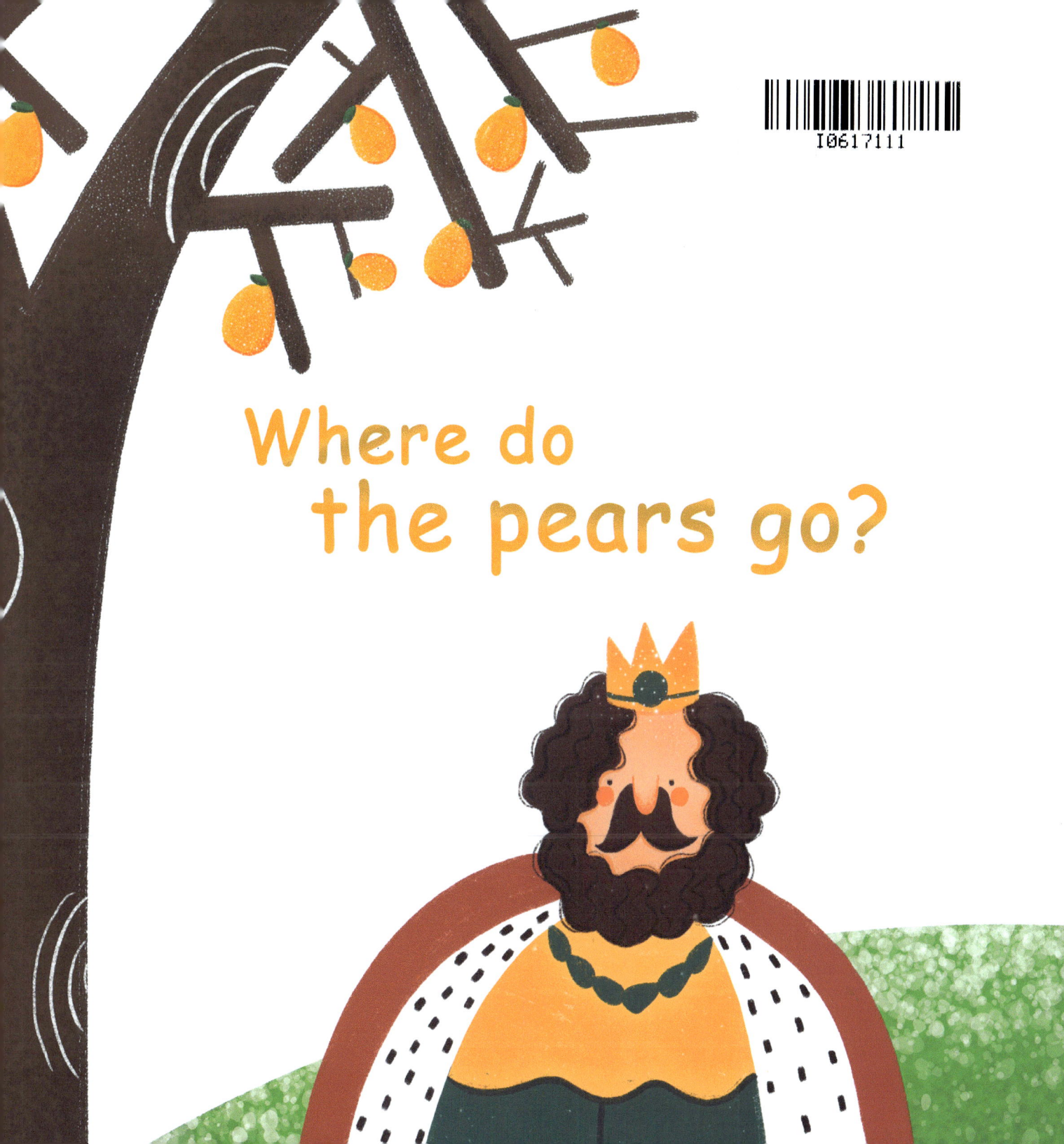

Where do the pears go?

Kidsocado Publishing House
Vancouver, Canada

Phone : +1 (833) 633 8654
WhatsApp: +1 (236) 333 7248
Email: info@kidsocado.com
https://kidsocadopublishinghouse.com

Serial Number: P2245250118

Title: Where Do the Pears Go?

Author: Nazila Roudini

Translator: Mohadeseh Roudini

Editor: Mohadeseh Roudini

Illustrator: Yeganeh Chekani

ISBN: 978-1-990760-63-1

Metadata: Junior Fiction, Social Themes

Book Size: 6.5 by 6.5 Inches

Pages: 34

Canada Publish Date: December 2022

Publisher: Kidsocado Publishing House

①

Once upon a time in faraway lands, a king lived with his three sons in a magnificent and large palace made of gold and emeralds.
But all this gold and jewelry is not what made the palace special.

②

③

Among all the things he did, the king loved gardening the most and went to his big garden every day and enjoyed the beautiful trees and flowers of the garden. The king loved the single pear tree in the middle of the garden among all the trees and flowers.
What was so special about this tree?

The pear tree always had pears, even in winter! The pears of this tree were golden, this was the king's secret, and no one knew about it.

Every morning when the king woke up, he visited his golden pear tree and took good care of it.

One morning, he woke up as usual and went to his garden to find that one of the pears was no longer golden! Worried and scared, he went to his palace and called all the palace servants; and told his minister to bring his sons to him.

When everyone came, the king asked them to take more care of the garden but did not say anything about his golden pears. He thought to himself: Who could pick my pears without permission?

Days passed by; and golden pears became food for birds and worms one after another.

The king became sadder every day; Until the king`s eldest son found out about this and asked the king to explain his unhappiness.

The king had to tell the boy the secret of his magic tree.

The older boy promised to protect the remaining golden pears soon.

He spent the whole day by the tree and did not allow the birds to climb the tree.

He raised a big umbrella on top of the tree to protect the pears from the wind and rain. But the next day, some of the pears lost their golden color.

The eldest son decided to ask his other brother for help. The next day, the two brothers tried to protect the golden pears, but they were still destroyed one by one.

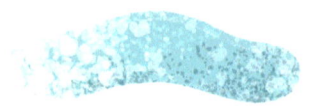

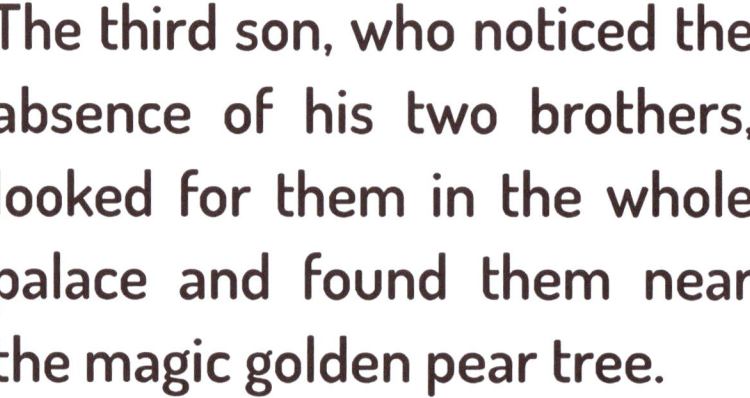

The third son, who noticed the absence of his two brothers, looked for them in the whole palace and found them near the magic golden pear tree. Two brothers shared the problem with him. The third brother started thinking. After thinking for a while, he said: "I will go to the Hakim and come back with a solution."

The boy quickly went to the house of the Hakim. When Hakim learned about the matter; He smiled and said: "Each tree keeps its fruit for a short time; before the fruits start to spoil and rot, they should be separated from the tree and planted next to the mother tree in the heart of the earth. But you should know that every fruit may not turn into a tree. Growing a tree requires a lot of effort and practice."

The boy, who had found the answer, returned to his brothers and the king and discussed the matter. But the king refused to pick golden pears.

23

Days passed one after the other, and every day more pears began to wither and rot; until only one golden pear remained on the tree. The third son could not bear his father's sadness and the destruction of the tree and pears; he went to the garden and picked the last pear.

Suddenly, the magical tree turned into dust and flew into the air. The boy, who was watching with surprise, realized that there was not much time left for the last golden pear to shine; he did not delay and started to dig a hole to plant the remaining golden pear. After making a hole in the ground, he put the pear in the soil and sprinkled water on it.

The king was angry when he learned about what his son had done. But the boy believed in his work. Every day, he visited the place where he planted the golden pear and treated them with water and fertilizer. Days passed without any sign, but the boy was hopeful with his efforts.

On one of these days, when he was going to water the buried golden pear, he saw a scene that he had been waiting for a long time. The golden pear had finally sprouted. He happily went to the king and his brothers and shared this happiness with them.

Months passed; the last golden pear had turned into a young tree. They knew already that they should turn the golden pears into golden pear trees before it was too late.

In the same way, the king's garden, which had only one magical tree, became a garden full of golden pears with the efforts of his sons and the others. People from other cities and countries traveled for months to visit these magical pears.

People of Golden Pearl City came to know that they should appreciate what they have and use it before it goes to waste. So, they can be happy and spread that happiness as far as they can.

The End.

Other Books from This Publishing House

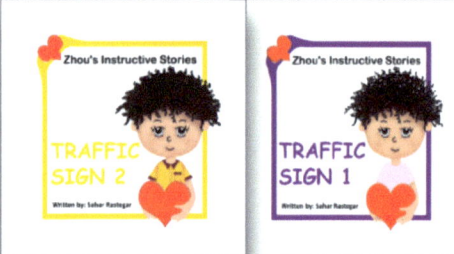

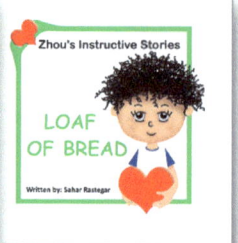

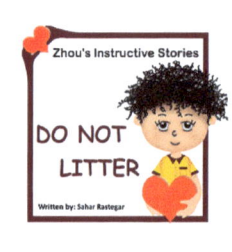
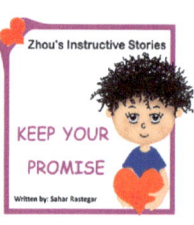
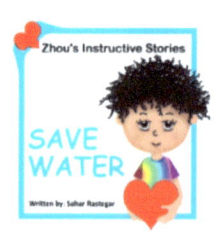

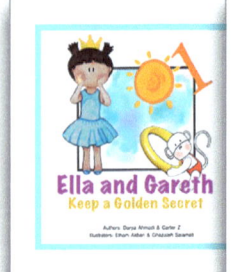
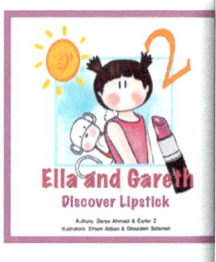

Access here:

www.ingramcontent.com/pod-product-compliance
Lightning Source LLC
Chambersburg PA
CBHW041619120626
46551CB00003B/503